Udoka M. Udoka

NIGERIA BEFORE AND AFTER AMALGAMATION

What went wrong, why and the way forward

This book is dedicated to the Almighty God.

Nigeria before and after amalgamation
What went wrong, why and the way forward

©2020 Udoka M. Udoka

print ISBN: 978-1-09833-884-8
ebook ISBN: 978-1-09833-885-5

CONTENTS

INTRODUCTION

1. Nations are created by God (Acts 17 vs 26) and countries are made by man. Before the advent of the colonial masters, nations of the earth had existed, made of one people and the bounds of their habitation. The colonial masters in their quest to acquire and establish colonies in Africa and other parts of the world engaged in the act of colonization over the indigenous people of an area. Colonization is the discovery of a large body of people existed by common descent, history, culture or language, inhabited a particular area, territory or state. When two or more of these nations are brought together it becomes a country. The bringing together of two or more nations to become a country is the hand work of colonization either with or without the consent of the individual nation is called 'Amalgamation'. Amalgamation means bringing or coming together of people of different nationalities that never had anything in common or any sacrament from Adam or creation to form a union for the reason of Bigger the Better. They must be independent, coming together to form a union (country) to be strong, stronger as a union to stand bold in the face of contemporary security challenges and other economic benefits. If the nations that form a country or are forced to form a country are independently

weak it becomes a weak country. Though, people of same or similar characteristics in terms of tradition, religion, culture, trade and organisations among others could form a union for same purposes of Bigger the Better, who are ideologically connected or otherwise. For instance, water, kerosene and oil can co-exist independently but will never mix to become one. The common denomination is that they all liquid but are made differently and have different purposes because of their inherent different characteristics. Therefore, a country is amalgamated to be united in terms of trade, defence and other benefits derivable from the union and presumably not as one or an entity.

2.   A nation could be likened to a Tree with a stem and many branches of different sizes and shapes. The stem represents the biggest tribe in a nation while the branches represent different dialects within the nation. The stem carries these different branches or dialects and supplies all their needs as one body in truth and faith, and they work together to achieve common goals, prosperity and development. When two or more nations are joined together for a purpose, each of these nations must stand independently though working together for a purpose beneficial to them. What could that purpose be "The Bigger the Better" When one of the nations wants to carry the rest on its shoulder what happens? Can a tree carry a branch as big as the stem? If it does what happens? The easiest answer that will come to mind is that it is bound to fall. Every nation on the earth created by God is created to stand on its own. If two or more nations want to work together they must work together based on common understanding and agreement for the purpose of Bigger the Better for enhanced economic development and national security. Do not lose the sight that "Smaller the Stronger""Together the Strongest"'

3. Globally, many nations were discovered and many countries were made by act of colonization by the colonial masters. In Africa and South America there are nations and countries within them. United States of America is a product of amalgamation of small percentage of different nations of the world for their development and national security for the reason of the Bigger the Better. A State is not a nation, kingdom or a country based on its formation. Every State in America is independent and a strong State and coming together to form a union makes America the strongest country in the world. Nations therein in South America include Brazil, Argentina, Peru, Venezuela among others are existing as created by God and on the principle of smaller the stronger. Similarly, in Europe there are countries and nations that made up Europe Union (EU). Examples of countries in Europe that are of significance to this book are United Kingdom (UK) and Spain. United Kingdom is composed of many nations namely England, Scotland, Wales (Great Britain) and Northern Island. These nations come together to form United Kingdom for the reason of bigger the better for enhanced national security and economic development. Some nations in Europe include: Italy, Germany, and France, among other existing independently on the principle of smaller the stronger.

4. In Africa, Nigeria and Tanzania are countries among others while Ghana, Sierra Leone, Congo, Senegal, Togo are nations among others. In Nigeria, the three ethnic nationalities or nations that made up the country existed at different time and space before the advent of colonial quest for territorial control and occupation in different parts of the world especially in Africa. The French colonialism dominated substantial parts of Africa and West Africa sub-region. British colonial masters after realising that West Africa was almost completely under the French colonisation quickly and hurriedly spurred into action and eventually discovered the three major ethnic nationalities that are called Nigeria today, the name which was born out of the major river in the sub-region called River Niger. These three (3) nationalities that made up Nigeria are Hausa, Ibo and Yoruba. These different nationalities existed independently in accordance with God's creation bounded by different geographical and climatic conditions.

5.   These three major ethnic nationalities or nations do not have anything in common or sacrament together from Adam. The human beings are different as well as the culture, religious beliefs, tradition, even type of food they eat and mode of eating are different, soil, and weather are totally different among others. These three nations after discovery were administered and controlled by the colonial administrators. In 1914, the sole administrator, Lord Lugard in his knowledge decided to amalgamate the three nations to become a country and he called it "Nigeria". Nigeria is a product of fear of the unknown so do other amalgamations or unions. His reason for the amalgamation was questioned by the British Council back at home. He responded that he did the amalgamation in good faith and for the interest of the three nationalities namely Hausa, Ibo and Yoruba. He further asserted that he was aware that they are different people but could be united for a purpose similar to that of the United Kingdom which is for Bigger the Better. Looking at their location in the West African sub-region is a big threat if allowed to exist independently. Nigeria is an island in the hands of French colonies. The threat was because they were surrounded by French colonies. If they are united or amalgamated it would be easier for them to stand any external aggression especially from the French colonies surrounding them also the size could be a

deterrence for would be invaders. The amalgamation was purely based on security (fear of the unknown) not solely on economic reasons as propounded by many scholars. Any attack on one is attack on all.

6. Furthermore, the amalgamation could help to boost their economic and technological development. The three nations would exist independently similar to that of the United Kingdom and administer their individual nations, contribute to the centre and run the country on the similar platform as the United Kingdom. This was the vision of the sole administrator in uniting the different nationalities to form a country called Nigeria. These nationalities were Eastern, Western and Northern regions of Nigeria. These three regions or nations were amalgamated and appropriate name for the amalgamation was not given to it. The appropriate name would have been "United Republic of Nigeria" which was a name propounded by Sir Lord Lugard but eventually dropped either because of lack of knowledge or ignorance. The word UNITED is a key word used to join different nations, kingdoms or states together. Looking at all the country of the world that were amalgamated or joined together, the word United preceded their names for example United State of America, United Kingdom, United Arab Emirate and United Republic of Tanzania among others. These countries were properly united, the reason for the unification was well understood by all and they work towards the vision for their unification.

7. The vision for the unification of Nigeria was in focus until Nigeria became independent in 1960. The notable political leaders then Sir Abubakar Tafawa Belewa, Dr. Nnamdi Azikiwe and Chief Obafemi Awolowo championed the course for independence without having a full grip or understanding of the vision for the amalgamation and eventually went their different ways in pursuit of their selfish agenda. This selfish agenda and lack of vision on their part led to what is today an incomplete name of a country called Nigeria which is at the brisk of collapse, poor governance, corruption, lack of free and fair election, insecurity, lack of spiritual intelligence, lack of national character, lack of knowledge in governance, lack of credible constitution, big gap between the rich and the poor, poverty, poor leadership, lack of management of key infrastructure, poor resource control, poor airport management, intimidation of the populace by the security agencies among others. The way forward will be to address some of the pertinent issues and challenges dating back to pre-independence, post-independence, what went wrong, why and strategies to correct them to bring the country on the right direction. To begin with the name of the country is inappropriate and should be renamed with all embracing name called "United Republic of Nigeria" for enhanced national security, peace and development. The three nations that made up Nigeria must be independent and working together at the centre for the common good of all for the reason of Bigger the Better.

PURSUIT OF SELFISH AGENDA

8.   This pursuit of selfish agenda by the political leaders had positioned the country well into the wrong direction that leads to doom. The leaders oblivious of the direction to steer the country have left the country completely at sea. There are two directions in live, the right direction that leads to destiny and the wrong direction that leads to doom. Unfortunately, Nigeria political leaders had since independence towed the part in the wrong direction that leads to doom. The Right direction that leads to destiny has only one track and the one that leads to doom in wrong direction has so many short cuts. Unfortunately, Nigeria has been steered well into the wrong direction that has so many short cuts with each regime since independence emerging from different short cuts in the wrong direction. That is why at the end of every regime the country is left worse that it met it. Forward never, Backward ever. This was the legacy the First Republic political leaders bequeathed to the next generations. They only succeeded in sowing the seeds of discord that grew up to bear un-edible fruits for the people of Nigeria. The present political leaders have also succeeded in building a very fragile country like a ten (10) story building built on a very weak foundation standing at almost 60 degrees (akimbo). The leaders never saw anything wrong with the building at 60 degrees and they are busy carrying out screeding, painting and furnishing of the building.

9.   This is a clear manifestation of the kind of mentality and knowledge of leadership our leaders possessed. This shows a clear disappointment and failure on the part of the leadership of Nigeria. The formation of the country called Nigeria was deliberate and requires deliberate understanding and agreement to make it work. Otherwise in trying to solve one problem out of the numerous problems the country have, another one will come up and it becomes a virtuous circle-problem unlimited with no credible solution. Therefore, to build a great country on a solid foundation for sustainable peace, development and progress the political leaders must shun the pursuit of selfish agenda, embrace love faith, true union in the true sense of it for enhanced national peace and development in Nigeria.

INSECURITY

10.   Insecurity is one of the greatest enemies of peace and development. It has gradually becoming a way of live in Nigeria. The citizens no longer care about it but to live their life in amidst insecurity. Nigeria as one of the most populous Black Country in the world has adopted a new way of live which is living in fear and insecurity. Insecurity emerges out of disunity. Where there is peace and security there is unity. A country is united voluntarily for a purpose and not forced to be united. In Nigeria several operations or security outfits have been created to force relative peace on the citizens. What this simply means is that all is not well with the country. Looking at the ugly trends of development and security in Nigeria today, it appears that the leadership and rest of the stakeholders are very much at home with what is happening in the country where poverty and insecurity rain supreme. Anywhere there is insecurity there must be a reason for that. There is no effect without cause. I think the right thing to do is to find out that which precipitated this' effect' which is insecurity and try to fashion out the best possible way to solve the 'cause' to build a better society for all and sundry. Adopting insecurity as a way of life is not a good legacy to be bestowed on the next generations of ours.

11. The entire world is becoming grossly insecure and every step must be taken to bring back peace and security in the world. It is only when there is peace and security that heaven and earth will be at peace with each other and the essence of creation which is LOVE would be actualized. There is this saying *"there will be greatest peace on earth if on every bad mouth a padlock is hung".* Insecurity begins with the tongue. Therefore there is the need for the political leaders and all stakeholders to retrace their steps, watch what they do and screen what they say. Where there is no LOVE, there is no PEACE. Therefore for Nigeria to live in peace the citizens must learn how to LOVE one another for enhanced national security, peace and development. Another reason why insecurity persist in some parts of Africa especially in Nigerians is because the political class, successful business men and privileged military officers surrounded themselves with armed security operatives both during and after official working hours and even up to retirement. So when the masses crying of insecurity, they pay little or no attention to the crying of the masses because they and their households and their businesses are well protected from the tax payers money. Taxes are paid for security and comfort of the citizens of a nation or country. The problem of insecurity will get desired attention only when personal security guards of limited number are restricted only to the Mr President and his Vice, while other entitled government functionaries' will only use personal security and drivers during office hours. With this law or policy in place everybody will begin to pay due attention to the problem of insecurity in Africa and Nigeria in particular. Furthermore, government needs to stop some people hiding under the guise of religion to perpetrate insecurity. This situation has reached a worrisome development, for example suicide bombers using hijab for deception among others. With this in place also the problem of corruption will drop approximately from 100 to 20 percent over night. The resultant effects will be growing attention to social amenities, employment, welfare services, peace and security.

12. Hijab - its implication to national security. Why Hijab is worn? In the days of Abraham with the moving away of the first children of Abraham from his household to desert environment, the nature of the environmental weather conditions prevalent in the desert, made the people of Ishmael to devised means to protect themselves, their hairs, ears and entire body from the scorch of the sand storm and other weather conditions associated with the desert. Hijab was primarily introduced for the protection of the head, hair and ears from sand storm. Hence the use of 'Hijab' to protect their hairs, ears and long gown to protect their body. Subsequently, over time and because of evil nature of man, people began to use its covert nature, capitalized on hijab as a means to cover their faces to propagate evil intension and for others as a custom to preserve an identity devoid of the reason for its inception. Today's contemporary security challenges some group of evil minded people adopted it as a means to perpetrate evil practices and export same to other parts of the world for same purposes.

13. Hijab was originally designed to be worn in the desert environment only because of desert weather situation and not to be worn elsewhere. Today it has been exported to Europe, USA, Asia and other parts of Africa where there is no desert condition. It has become a mode of dressing outside the desert areas for a purpose. Therefore, it is incumbent on world political leaders to stand their grounds and restrict Hijab to be worn in areas where there is desert encroachment. Subsequently, people began to use it as a means to propagate false sense of culture and as a means to indoctrinate younger generation across the world that Hijab is a way to life which is obviously not the case. It is also used to introduce disharmony among people of different believe, culture and create distrust among them. It is important that people begin to tell people the true situation of things about life rather than giving false reason about life. It is only when people begin to teach people about the true essence of life, the way to live that life will be more meaningful to all, and there will be peace and harmony across the globe. Therefore, to minimize PBIED there is the need to abolish the wearing of Hijab outside the desert environment for enhances peace and national security.

POOR LEADERSHIP

14. Poor leadership has remained the bane for corruption and under development among others. Who is a leader? How are leaders made? How do leaders see their subjects, the people they lead? How do the people look up to their leaders? These questions demand genuine answers. In lives generally, there is a reason why God created man and woman and appointed man as the head, father or leader. This appointment or selection is but for a purpose and it's quite unfortunate that the essence or objective of the appointment is not always followed, adhered to or understood by many in most countries of the world particularly in Africa. This is one of the main reasons that African countries are grossly underdeveloped, poorly governed and are laden or wallowing in abject poverty and lack of civilization. Looking at what is happening in Africa today one would begin to wonder whether Africa is a caused continent. Obviously no, because Africa is richly blessed by God in terms of human, mineral resources and climatic balance yet the people are not utilizing the endowment bestowed on the continent in the right direction. This is one of the reasons Africa is suffering today.

15. In the developed countries like US, UK and Russia among others the stories are different because their leaders have established an enduring platform to keep their countries on the right track in the right direction. This is what made them today to be the choice countries for all. In African countries like South Africa, Egypt, Sudan and Nigeria among others the situation is different, the environment is good and richly blessed yet their citizens are living in abject poverty, corruption, nepotism, insecurity, hatred and poor governance. Social lives and harmonious existence are virtually non-existent. In Nigeria since independence, the people have never witnessed or known what is called good standard of living in terms of peace, security, social lives and development.

16. The political leaders since independence to present have always seen themselves differently from the people they lead. They see themselves as winners take it all without recourse to the people. They have so much established the country in the wrong direction that leads to doom. This is why today the seeds of discord they sowed are what the citizens are ripping at present. The fathers, the political masters and leaders from the past to present have no credible legacy for the citizens and the generations to come. It is quite unfortunate that these leaders perish because of lack of knowledge and wisdom to put the country on the right pedestal. A good father, leader or administrator is measured after he has ruled and gone, the legacy he left behind him is worthy of mentioning from generation to generation. Like our elders used to say "*a tree is best measured when it is down*". Therefore, there is need for political leaders/fathers to endeavour to leave behind good legacies for posterity, for enhance peace, security and national development.

17. Things do not happen for nothing. There is a reason behind everything that happens. Therefore, to see the reason why things happen the way they happen it is mandatory to find out the reason why it is happening and try to get to the root cause of the problem and nib it in the bud instead of running around it in the name of solving it. That problem will never be solved. It can only provide temporary solution and will reappear after a while. It is said that it is only what you know and understand very well you can fix, maintain and possibly repair. From all intent and purposes, Nigerians do not know and understand the country they live in hence the confusion all the time. A true leader takes some time to analyze every event to find out the reason for the cause and effect of that event before venturing to solve the problem. A leader must not act at the spur of the moment but rather takes his time to study the reason for the cause and effect. A leader must not approach issues with a bias mind. Any situation that is approached with a bias mind gets a bias solution which ultimately gets condemnation from right thinking people or the general public. Most leaders fail in their class of leadership because of the way they handle issues of national significance without recourse to the reason for the cause and effect. Therefore, there is the need for political leaders to look at issues with an objective mind and endeavour to solve it objectively for enhance peace and national security.

POVERTY

18.   Poverty is a measure of how poorly a country is governed. It is also a measure of perseverance on the part of individuals or citizens concerned. To be POOR is a TEST and to be RICH is also a test. Both RICH and POOR are complementary and are not permanent depending on the understanding of the people. They are dated back to the beginning of time of mankind for a purpose. God has a reason for His creation of mankind and a purpose for making some poor and some rich. The reason is not farfetched. When a man is poor it simply means that God made him poor to test his obedience and loyalty to his creator and most often than not the POOR always FAIL the test. They fail because of lack of understanding and knowledge. They go about engaging themselves into activities that are not of God to become rich. To be poor is a test because no condition is permanent. Poverty could become prosperity by simply working hard through research and development, praying and trusting in God. At the appointed time, having passed the test of obedience and loyalty to God the poor becomes sustainably rich and happier in life.

19. While to be RICH in its true sense is also a test from God. God made man rich to test his obedience and loyalty to Him. Similarly, the rich fall because they forget Him that made them rich and want to sustain or become richer thereby engaging themselves into some activities that put them in direct opposition with God. Some of these activities include corruption, rituals, occultism and greediness among others. These failures of the rich and the poor adversely affect the determination and development of a nation and by extension a country. A country could become poorer or richer depending on their understanding and approach to divine providence. Therefore, there is the need for poor nations, poor countries, rich nations and rich countries to work hard and wait on the Lord for sustainable peace, security and development.

POOR GOVERNANCE

20. Poor governance is one of the major bad attributes that destroys a nation and a country. Poor governance happens the way they happen because of lack of knowledge on the part of the leaders. What this means is that when things go wrong in the governing process but because of lack of knowledge the political leaders would try to use wrong approach to correcting that which is wrong. By so doing they end up compounding the wrong the more. The resultant effect is thereby creating instability in the polity which eventually results to break down of law and order. There is a distinct relationship between the laws of social sciences and law of science. In social/applied sciences you use right approach to correct wrong procedures to achieve desired result. This statement can be simplified by using mathematical method: which means using positive against negative gives you positive results. Similarly, using negative approach against wrong procedure gives you greater negative results:

$$+ \text{ against } - = +$$

$$- \text{ against } - = > -$$

Law of science - That is, like poles repel whereas unlike poles attract.

Furthermore, in law of political /social sciences you use right (+) approach to improve on right procedures and negative approach to compound negative procedures to get further negative results.

What these simply mean is that:

$$+ \text{ against } + = >+$$

$$- \text{ against } - = >-$$

Therefore, law of social/political sciences is inversely proportional to law of science.

Whereas, in mystical science, like poles attract while unlike poles repel.

Positive force(+) against Negative force(-) = Repel

Positive force(+) against Positive force(+) = Attract

Negative force(-) against Negative force(-) = No action

From this analysis, it therefore follows that laws of sciences are inversely proportional to laws of mystical sciences. Therefore in every aspect of life these laws hold true in either cases. In advance countries like US, UK and France among others these laws are well understood and judiciously applied both in politics and other aspects of human endeavours.

21. Furthermore, things happen the way they happen in governance in Nigeria simply because of the adoption of wrong procedures and approaches in governance. There is this saying that says *"Jack of all trade masters of none"*. Putting round pegs in square holes is ultimately a serious setback in governance in Nigeria. This system of governance in Nigeria has adversely hampered economic, political, technological, social security, national development and threatened the unity and peaceful co-existence of Nigerian people. Nigeria is one of the few backward countries in the world today that uphold this wrong principle. That is to say that the country is sinking without knowing because of lack of knowledge and understanding that the system of government that it is practicing is bad. This system is leading the country in the wrong direction that leads to doom. Nigeria is a country of approximately 180million people with diverse nationalities, ethnicity, tradition and religion among others. In Nigeria, the lives, policing, protection of life, administration, challenges of both local and foreign issues, protection of sovereignty and territorial integrity rest on the shoulder of one man, the President. It is practically impossible for such country or countries to effectively manage and correct one aspect of its numerous problems. Jack of all trades, Masters none.

22. This system has been on for more than 50 years in Nigeria yet its political leaders could not read the hand writing on the wall that all is not well with the country. This is a very serious flaw in the system of government in Nigeria and requires total overhaul. The best approach to solving these problems is to go back to the drawing board and fashion out the best way forward just as it is being practiced in most developed countries of the world such as US, UK and China where the states, regions and nations that come together to constitute a country are made to administer, manage, govern themselves and form a union for the reason of the Bigger the Better. These nations that unite to form a country make certain percentages according to their buoyancy to the centre to handle internal and external issues and challenges. These by so doing will reduce stress on the country's Leaderships for enhanced national security and development. Therefore, for Nigeria to survive as a country there is the need to borrow a system that has been tested and certified appropriate for national survival and development as being practices in US and UK among others which is "True Federalism or Confederation System of Government or Parliamentary System" which will reposition the country on the right direction to destiny for enhanced national security and development.

23. Furthermore, it is the responsibility of the government at the centre to handle issues, agendas that have national, international significance rather than complicating, compounding issues and agendas which have ultimately left the country completely at sea. It pays to live in a country where good governance reigns supreme rather than living a country where all evil thrives as a result of poor governance that takes pre-eminence. It is important to note that division of labour provide ample opportunity for research and development, better security, supervision and by extension good governance for enhanced national security and development.

ISSUES OF POLITICAL APPOINTMENT FREE AND FAIR ELECTION

24. Politics is the use of intrigues, actions and strategies that are employed in obtaining any position of power or control in a government or to influence or maneuver a government decisions to ones advantage. Election is a process of electing or choosing individuals to oversee the affairs of an organization or government offices in a particular setting in government, business or organisations. This process is not strictly followed that is why things are not properly done or put to achieve desired results. In developed countries, election is used to elect a set of individuals to govern the people for a predetermined period of time and so on and it is a vicious circle. In Africa, this process is not duly applied to elect individuals into established government ministries, department and agencies. In Nigeria since inception elections had never been seen as free and fair and as a result wrong individuals have always been elected to occupy government offices. What this simply means is "putting square pegs in round holes". Electing people that are not worthy in character and learning to occupy public offices. People who do not know anything about the country they want to govern.

25. Free and Fair elections in politics is a matter that requires serious attention. From the obvious political process, incessant misconceptions of electoral outcomes that eventually resulted to loss of lives and property showed that our political leaders and electorates do not understand the meaning of "Free and Fair" election in politics. This is one of the major reasons why every election in Nigeria was always characterized with violence since inception. Looking at elections in more developed countries especially in US, UK and China among others, there is always a near non-significant post election violence in these countries. What this means is that there is better understanding of the word "Free and Fair" which some of the political class in Africa especially in Nigeria are oblivious of. Therefore there is the need to properly wise up our so called political juggernauts in Nigeria through orientation and education.

26. 26.Consequently, let me use this opportunity to tell our political leaders and electorates that what "Free and Fair" election means first and foremost is that Fair as a grade is at the lowest threshold in the right direction.

  a. Fair as the least grade

  b. Satisfactory

  c. Good

  d. Very Good

  e. Excellent as the peak in the right direction.

What this simple means is that human nature is not devoid of malpractice and human beings are not perfect. Because human beings are not perfect therefore there is no election anywhere in the world including the advanced countries that goes without malpractices but the malpractice would be within some acceptable limit for it to be acceptable as "Free and Fair". The Western world and United States of America among others understood this electoral principle and that is why there is almost non-significant post election violence in those countries. Perfect or Excellent election is only possible in Heaven not on Earth. Therefore, there is the need for Nigerians to re-orient themselves and walk on the path of reality in the right direction for enhanced political stability and national security.

SPIRITUAL INTELLIGENCE

27. Spiritual Intelligence is the process whereby knowledge is gained in the supernatural process for use in the physical. Spirituality opens doors for scientific, technological and all forms of human social development to manifest in the physical. This is why most of the advanced countries in the world keyed into spirituality to acquire knowledge for scientific, technological and economic development for enhanced national security. They do this by organizing highly gifted citizens into cells to research into the spiritual world for answers to issues bordering on the needs of the country.

28. There are four (4) different types or stages of spirituality namely Mundane Spiritual Intelligence, Strategic Spiritual Intelligence, Universal Spiritual Intelligence and Supreme Spiritual Intelligence. These forms of spirituality operate at different realm and space.

    a.   **Mundane Spiritual Intelligence.** Mundane Spiritual Intelligence is the type of local spiritual activities that operate at the lower level with no significant impact on scientific, technological and human development. They are mostly used by locals to perpetrate wrongs in the society.

b. **Strategic Spiritual Intelligence**. Strategic Spiritual Intelligence is the type that operates at the atmospheric level at a higher realm in space. They are usually used to obtain limited knowledge for use in scientific, technological and human development. The group that are involved in this type of spirituality often times combine it with mundane spiritual process thereby limiting their scope of knowledge.

c. **Universal Spiritual Intelligence.** Universal Spiritual Intelligence is another level of spirituality that is called Universal Spiritual Intelligence. This realm of spirituality is above all other forms of spirituality next to Supreme Spiritual Intelligence. For you to exist in this form you must be spiritually endowed from heaven and you will have the privileges to see and hear from Supernatural Beings that's God and Angels of God. You also have the powers to fight demonic forces, influences and can employ the services of Angels in the fight against evil forces. This is the highest form of spirituality attained by humans. This form of spirituality transcends time. Only very few people about two per cent of the world population that are experiencing this special power (Gift) and privileges on earth. They have the powers to visit the spiritual world to see who they want to see and get information they want. They also have powers to heal, see vision and cast out demons. This is absolute divine gift to mankind, a spiritual knowledge ever attained.

d. **Supreme Spiritual Intelligence**. Supreme Spiritual Intelligence is divine in nature and it provides all inclusive knowledge, wisdom and understanding. It opens doors to unlimited scientific, technological and human development. It guarantees peace and security in all its ramifications. It is a sure process of spirituality and life. This is the type that is recommended for all nations. It is for God alone. In live, the earth is divided into 360 degrees so is human paths to destiny. Every creature toes a path of destiny out of the 360 degrees. Along each path, one is expected to meet on its path the good, the bad and the ugly. And these different types of human beings you meet on your path shape your path to destiny either in the positive or negative direction. Your ability to overcome the bad and the ugly on your path depends on your personal relationship with the God Almighty for a just person, while others depend on their relationship with their personal gods. Remember the world population and the number of people that you will meet on your 360 degrees path. Everyone you meet on your path of live is destined to meet with you and degree of their impact to your live equally varies.

STATE OF MIND

29. Human mind operates in 360 degrees channels with its corresponding frequencies. Each channel has its corresponding frequency. For any event to happen one must tune to a particular frequency in the 360 degrees channels. Examples of channels are channels of violence, corruption, declaration of war or peace, and insecurity such as robbery, kidnapping and insurgency as well as channels of love and good or bad. For an individual to exhibits any of these channels he or she must tune to a particular frequency in the channels. For each channel to be active, at least two persons must be involved and tuned to the same frequency in the channels to make an event to happen be it love, good or bad event. For example, it must take two of like minds to be in the particular channel of frequency of love for true love and sweet fun to take place. Similarly, it must take two to be in a particular channel of frequency of hatred and accusations and counter accusations to be in the frequency of cosmetics of war for war or attack to be declared. Therefore, everybody's behaviour and character are drawn from these 360 degrees channels of frequencies for love, good or bad event to happen.

30. In Nigeria, the citizens are not known for any particular spiritual process. A country where spirituality is so mixed up that it almost difficult to separate Pauls from Banabas, the good from bad. A country where it is almost impossible to achieve meaningful objectives unlike other developed countries of the world where there is distinct separation of people in different levels of spirituality for specific purposes. In this part of the world it is like bringing sheep, goat and pigs together to dwell in the same den without proper demarcation which makes it more difficult to achieve any meaningful progress. While one is working others are pulling it down. At the end they remain stagnated with no hope to moving forward. This is a typical case with Nigeria among others.

31. What this simply means is that to move out of the stagnation and for the different people with different ideology and mentality to dwell in the same den bounded by the same international boundary must be distinctly separated within the boundary. The three (3) different nations must be separated to work independently of each other to harness their individual spirituality for scientific, technological and economic development. Each should be allowed to develop at its own pace to build a formidable nation and converge to the centre to showcase a powerful country comparable to any other in the world. In other words to bring lion, tiger and leopard into one den without defined boundaries is suicidal. They will never work for the common good of all. Therefore there is the need for the North, East and West to be on their own or independent but united at the centre for enhanced spiritual growth for scientific, technological and economic development in the United Republic of Nigeria.

FEDERAL / NATIONAL CHARACTER

32. Federal/National Character Commission was introduced to reduce some of the injustices in Nigeria to a reasonable extent. This national character is not reasonably practice in the country due to the inherent awkward character of some sections of the country who do not believe in equity and justice. The commission instead of serving the purpose for which it was created now it is dividing the country further into ethnic, religious, and tribal lines. There are lot of injustices in the country which makes one to wonder whether Nigeria will ever be good. There are lots of political instability ranging from state inequity, local government, political appointments, infrastructure distributions, promotion in military and other security agencies, selection into the military and other agencies, employment at the federal level as well as uneven distribution of federal fund at the so-state and local government levels among others.

33. The question now is – why is it that it is only in the National Assembly that we have a near resemblance of federal character? Why is it that national character as it were is never applied in the ministries, departments and agencies including the military? Promotion in MDA,

Military and political appointments do not in any way reflect the so called federal/national character for peace and equity. These inequalities are the major reasons why the country is at the brisk of collapse; many agitations here and there for restructuring, decentralization, autonomy and total separation. The country is becoming hopeless for the nations that made up Nigeria. Is this the right way in the right direction? Is this the legacy that we want to bequeath to the future generations? There is something that is fundamentally wrong with the amalgamation which needs to be looked into to redirect the country in the right direction. Lord Lugard meant well for uniting the nations that is today called Nigeria (though for fear of the unknown). Our quest for selfish agenda and lack of knowledge on the part of our so called political leaders had tampered with the foundation laid by Lord Lugard. The structure of the country had since then been standing at 60 degrees akimbo which is most likely to collapse at any time soon. There is no gain pretending that we are together when we are not. We are only busy slowing down each other's progress and development. If the three nations that made up Nigeria cannot work together for the vision of Lord Lugard which is not significant any longer in the current setting. The union should be dissolved for peace, security and development. The separation can be achieved through dialogue, peaceful, and cordial manner without loss of human life and property. The country can be separated and the nations remain friendly rather than being enemies. The way it stands now there is no light at the end of the tunnel except there is a total u-turn back to 1914 stand point in the democratic process in Nigeria for enhanced peace and development in the country.

THE WAY FORWARD

34. A government must be seen to run on Love, Trust and not on ethnic divide. It must be based on verification and authentication of issues and ideas that are of national interest and the interest of the citizenry. A leader must always verify and authenticate any intelligence received. He must convert it to actionable information before a directive for action is given as appropriate. It is only on this principle that a government is seen to be on the right side in the right direction in governance. To achieve this noble principle, the political leaders and the citizens must be seen to be constantly referring to the second law of God which says *"Love your neighbour as thy self"*. This is the only Law of God which if adequately followed by all and sundry will return the world to the very essence of creation in the right direction. The issues of love for oneself and love on tribal lines are the key foundations for corruption. Love of money is root of all evil. People put their life on firing line because of love of money. Love your neighbour as thyself will pave way for the exit of all kinds of evil vices in government, high degree of normalcy will return and cordial relationship between man and animals will be fostered.

35. In furtherance to this, you must do to others as you wish others to do unto you. It is only then that there will be the greatest peace, unity and progress again in the country. The country will become a joyful and God's praising garden that houses different creeds, tribes, nations, colours and religious among others. To achieve these in the country today there are issues of grave importance that need to be appropriately addressed for enhance peace, unity, progress and national security in Nigeria. Some of these key issues are constitution overhaul (restructuring), regional autonomy, state constitution, federal constitution as applicable to the centre and state police among others. This system of government will absolve the country from internal wrangling, monopoly of power, injustice, corruption, nepotism and insecurity among others. There are many countries in the world that imbibe this separation of power, create less jack of all trades masters none and are doing very great for instance United States of America (US), United Kingdom (UK), United Arab Emirate (UAE), China and United Republic of Tanzania among others that have similar or greater diversity than Nigeria.

36. For any meaningful progress and development to happen in Nigeria, Nigeria needs to shelve herself from the unfortunate system of government she is practicing that is detrimental, directionless and move to a more direct, transparent and purposeful system which is "CONFEDERATION" which means union of different nations to form a country for the purpose of Bigger the Better. They will operate on the principle of smaller the stronger but bounded or united on the basis of Bigger the Better. They will operate as independent nations and united at the centre as it is done in US, UK, and UAE among others which will give her the opportunity to stand out as one united and powerful country in Africa and comity of nations.

CONSTITUTION OVERHAUL

37. The constitution overhaul is the process by which the constitution is re-written to meet the aspiration of the citizens of that country and nation. The constitution of Nigeria as it were is on one side of the fence while the aspiration of the citizenry is on the other side. The constitution is not serving the people but only a few political smugglers who fashioned and operated the constitution to suit their political ambition to the detriment of the country. The constitution of Federal Republic of Nigeria as it is today is neither federal nor republic, directionless and very un-purposeful that is why it is not obeyed or yielding any useful results. It is quite amazing that at this period of 21 Century, Nigeria is finding it difficult to review the constitution to the benefit of all the nations that made up the country. When you chart a course that is obviously not leading you to anywhere, it is customary that you have to pause and ask yourselves where are we heading to? What is it that we are doing wrong? What is the best way forward? It is only then that you have to have a re-think and fashion out a new, more direct and purposeful constitution that is directional for peace, harmony and national security which is a perquisite for national development.

38. To achieve this ultimate goal for peace, security and national development, the country would have to have a role model constitution to be adopted because they want to live together as one united country for the purpose of Bigger the Better, Together the Strongest, greater economic development, greater influence in Africa and in the world at large. The country is recommended to adopt either the Untied States of America or United Kingdom Constitutional platform to safe the country from total collapse which is eminent. There is this adage that says *if you know your problem then you have solved it 50 percent.* The remaining 50 percent is putting in motion the strategy to bring it to a completion. When you don't know where the rain begins to beat you, you will never know where it stops. This is only possible when you have a good vision that is capable of carrying you into the future for enhanced peace, security and national development. Therefore, Nigeria should dissolve her 1999 Constitution as amended and empower the three region or the six geo-political zones whichever is convenient to evolve their constitutions as peculiar to the regions/ zones while the centre will formulate a constitution re-uniting the nations for the purpose of the Bigger the Better, Together the Strongest for enhanced peace, security and national development. Where it is not possible because of lack of vision, separation is the ANSWER.

REGIONAL AUTONOMY

39. *Regional Autonomy* – Regional autonomy is simply means granting the regions relative independence to be able to handle and administer issues and challenges affecting the region. These issues and challenges could come in the form of, but not limited to resource control, regional constitution, state police, state and rural infrastructure and administration among others. The major problem in the world today is the decision of certain group of people who are bent in denying others the right to peaceful existence because of greed.

40. This relative independence or autonomy would provide the regions ample opportunity to re-structure, reconstruct, reunify, united in their quest for research and development of their regions according to their own pace. It will equally enable them to venture into comprehensive real estate, science and technology. It opens up greater impetus for further research into the mineral resources available and their potentials for the development of their respective regions, improve their socio-cultural, political, economic and management of their citizenry. The regions as a matter of necessity make available certain percentage of their yearly income to the central government in accordance with their constitution. This is the only way forward for Nigeria to be able to harness her full potential to ensure peace, unity and development. Therefore there is the need for de-centralisation and granting the regions full autonomy for enhanced economic development and national security.

CONFEDERATION/DE-CENTRALISATION OF NIGERIA

41. Confederation/De-centralisation is a league or alliance or union of nations that are allowed or have the autonomy to manage and administer their internal affairs exclusively. This process of governance if granted would reduce undue pressure to the federal government as it were. It will enable the federal government to concentrate on those issues, activities and responsibilities that will enable it to achieve sustainable peace and development for enhanced national security. The federation as it were does not provide peace, security and development instead it encourages gradual decay and total insecurity.

42. Confederation/De-centralisation would help Nigeria to achieve, recover from her total decadence and regain her lost glory in the comity of nations. De-centralisation would ensure speedy development in terms of science and technology, better economic recovery and better lives for the citizens. It would give the central government the ample time and space to concentrate on fewer government policies that are of international significance. There would be less pressure on central government, less jack of all trades, less masters of none and less insecurity in the country. It will provide the central government longitude and latitude for the mastery of both internal and external environment. Therefore, there is the need to confederate/de-centralise the regions for enhance national development and security in Nigeria.

STATE OF THE UNION AND NOT STATE OF THE NATION

43. Nigeria as a country is a conglutination of nations that came together to form the country called Nigeria which otherwise suppose to be known as "UNITED REPUBLIC OF NIGERIA". But because of some political intrigues by some mischievous citizens decided to abandon the proposed name for Nigeria and called the country Nigeria without any prefix attached. An attempt by some well meaning Nigerians to go back to the proposed name by Lord Lugard was unsuccessful hence they rather opted for the Federal Republic of Nigeria in 1963 when the country became a republic. This political intrigues has today derailed the original plan for the amalgamation (union) involving the East, the West and the North. This union was originally done for the purpose of the Bigger the Better for defence and other benefits such as trade and economic development. Today the North is taking the advantage that the word United is missing in the name of the country and assiduously working to over-run the East and West regions of Nigeria. This unholy attitude is not only setting the pace of development of the country backward but it will also destroy the vision of Lord Lugard for the amalgamation (union).

The reason for coming together was to defend any attack from any of the Francophone countries surrounding the country within the West Africa Sub-region and also for economic and scientific development. Any attack on any of the nations in Nigeria is attack on all. Therefore for Nigeria to survive as a country, it must revert back to the intended name which is United Republic of Nigeria for all the nations in it to have sense of belonging. These nations will be independent and working together for greater and stronger Nigeria.

NATION KINGDOM STATE COUNTY COUNTRY: RELATIONSHIP BETWEEN THEM

44. The fundamental relationship between Nation, Kingdom, State, County and Country: First and foremost, there are only two recognized English languages in the world namely British and American English languages. Depending on which side of the divide you are determines the applicability of the word in English. On the British side, British refer to Nation as Kingdom tracing its origin from their traditional heritage. On the American side, America call an assemblies of small percentage of different nationalities a State according to their traditional heritage. It therefore follows that Kingdom = Nation from the first principle that is creation. Nations are created by God. Countries and States are made by man. Nations and Kingdoms are the same depending on the traditional heritage while countries and States are different and are made by man. For clear understanding, you have to know how each of them (country or state) is made. A country is made when you have two or more nations or kingdoms coming together to form a Union for the reason of the bigger the better for the purpose of trade and ultimately for defence which is called amalgamation.

For example, United Kingdom, Spain, United Republic of Tanzania and Nigeria among others. A prefix United must precede the name of the amalgamated nations or kingdoms called a country. A State is when a small percentage or fraction of different races, colors, creed, traditions, languages, religions, cultures and people among others are migrating or migrated to a particular location or locations at the same time in space. It is called a State when the people are grouped for easy administration and governance. A vivid example of where such migration had happened is in America hence United States of America among others. It is absolutely wrong and utterly ridiculous, mischievous and disorderly for any group of people to call amalgamation of different nations wherein the constituents are people of the same nations or kingdoms are people of same tribe, race, religious beliefs, tradition, culture among others, a State. It completely shows lack of knowledge, and understanding of terms of words to be used by such people who called a nation, a state and a country, a State. This misrepresentation is the bases of or foundation of corruption and insecurity in some parts of the world and Africa in particular today where many people thrive in the midst of confusion and disorder. Every nation or kingdom is giving a specific boundary for their own existence having almost everything in common from Adam or Adamic linage. Whereas Countries and States are made by man NOT GOD for specific purposes. God has no direct bearing in the making of a country or a state as it is sole responsibility of man to amalgamate or form a union or club of nations and states depending on their agreement, knowledge and understanding of the reality of the moment at the time. Two things are involved in a union called amalgamation for the purpose of the bigger the better, one is trade and other is defence. For instance, United Kingdom is made up of four Kingdoms they are

England, Wales, Scotland and Northern Ireland. England, Wales and Scotland are British known as Great Britain, while Northern Ireland is Irish. They got together in a union for the reason of the bigger the better for trade and defence. Whereas America is made of 50 States comprised of small percentage of every nation of the world commonly referred to as States by Americans.

45. This union of Kingdoms or Nations and States is called amalgamation for the purpose of Free Trade that knows No Trade Protocol. The underlining factor behind the screen in for the union called amalgamation is DEFENCE. Subsequently, for ease of administration, these nations, kingdoms or states are subdivided into Counties for ease of local administrative authorities. It therefore follows that when two or more nations or kingdoms and states agreed to come together to form a union called amalgamation for the purpose of the bigger the better for trade and defence among others, it becomes a COUNTRY. This union or amalgamation is always prefix with word 'United' preceding the name of the country for example United Kingdom. United States, United Arab Emirate, United Republic of Tanzania among others. This union is not limited to nations and states but could be extended to nations and countries combined as it is with European Union (EU) and former USSR.

46. In Nigeria, Nigeria is made up of three (3) nations as the case may be namely Easter Nigeria (Republic of Biafra), Western Nigeria (Oduduwa Republic and Northern Nigeria (Republic of Arewa). These three nations were amalgamated by Sir Lord Lugard in 1914 for the same purpose of the bigger the better for trade and defence bearing in mind that these nations are islands or surrounded by French speaking nations or colonies for ease of trade and protection. In case of any attack from any of the French colonies to any of the nations in Nigeria it will be an attack on all. Today, these three nations are commonly referred to as Arewa in the North, Oduduwa in the West and Biafra in the East. These three nations are what made up United Republic of Nigeria a name that was pencilled or suggested by Sir Lord Lugard but was lost in transit to independence in 1960 for mischievous reasons. Consequently, after the Nigeria – Biafra war from 1967 to 1970 with No Victor, No Vanquish. The military authorities at that time in a bid to further disorganized the union or amalgamation planned to embarked on divide and rule orchestrated by Northern group (Arewa) against Biafra and Oduduwa republic with the sole intent to re-colonise them. This plan of divide and rule for easy colonization resulted to sub-dividing nations into COUNTIES and called it States because of lack of knowledge, understanding and ignorance. The gospel truth is either they did not know the true meaning of the words nations and states or want to remain in ignorance.

47. Nigeria is made up of three nations and not so-called 36 states. Half education is dangerous as it was common within the leadership circle at that time, present and into the future. The so called elites at the time and present could not offer useful advice hence the country's continuous political problems. Calling a county a state is not only ridiculous but also shows lack of knowledge and understanding as it is widely said that my "people perish because of lack of knowledge." These deception, deceit and destruction pervading the entire country ranging from different sizes and shapes right from inception are the bane of corruption plaguing the country today, lack of leadership qualities, lack of development, lack of good governing processes which bread frequent violence in all its ramifications leading to insurgency and subsequent agitations from all sides for disintegration of the Union called amalgamation for peace and security in Nigeria. The country can only move forward when the leaders and citizens accept the Reality of the moment. Accepting the Reality of the moment means you have good knowledge of the situation. Having good knowledge of the situation, shows you have true understanding of the situation from the first principle. Therefore, knowledge and understanding are the keys of the Reality of the moment for advancement in all facets of life for enhance peace and national security.

THE MIDDLE-BELT REGION

48. The Middle-Belt region since pre-independence era has been an independent region characterized mainly of minor tribes and dialects within its geographical boundary in Nigeria. This region, because of political convenience was ceded to the North by the British colonial masters for the purpose of easy administration and political advantage to the North during amalgamation. This region was predominantly Christian minority but ceded to Muslim majority north who saw it as an advantage to use them as footstool to achieve their political game against the East and West. Today the middle beltians having identified that the north only required them for political dominance as fashioned by the colonial masters against other blocs in the country. Because of this obvious advantage, the north continued to marginalized the region in every respect in other not for the region to be politically strong to have a say in the scheme of things in Nigeria. The middle beltians realizing their predicament sought to fight for their self realization and determination which has further compounded their political stance and strained their fragile relationship with the north. The north is not comfortable with their political agitations, hence had no option than to decimate, destroy them physically, politically, eventually take over full control of the region and Islamize them for greater northern Nigeria. They employ this by using militias such as Boko Haram and herdsmen. Hence what is happening to the entire region today has changed the political landscape of Nigeria for unexpected to happen.

49. This political upheaval has continued to claim lives and property in the region and by extension other parts of the country. This problem has for a very long time lingering without a corresponding check by the so-called political elites in the country. This is why up till now the situation seems unrecoverable because the so-called elites are completely at sea as to what needs to be done for immediate recovery. Yet they refused to call MAY DAY or declare state of emergency in the country for external assistance. It is quite unfortunate that their mischievous minds are the bane of this confusion which have plunged the Republic into a perpetual nose dive. Until the proper needful is done there will be no light at the end of the tunnel. Hence the Republic is already well established on the extended line for immediate touch down on the wrong direction that leads to doom. Therefore, there is the need for the elders, stakeholders, and so called political masters to rally round on a round table to double check their plotted courses of actions and intended direction for the country before it is too late. As our old adage has it that "a stich in time saves nine".

For example, UK started with the amalgamation of union of four nations starting with trades and technologies among others from their neighbouring nations which metamorphous in to one United Kingdom comprising of England, Scotland, Wells and Northern Island for the same reason of the Bigger the Better. This union was primarily for trade and later for defence in case of external aggression on the constituted members of the union. It started as a simple trade union as far back in 1886 and later amalgamated for protection of common interests and defence. The End justifies the Means; therefore the primary intention for the amalgamation of United Kingdom was for defence.

NATION POLICE AND NATIONAL SECURITY IN NIGERIA

50. Societies worldwide need peaceful and stable environment for the provision and sustenance of security. It is under such a secured society that the nation could mobilise both its human and materials resources for any meaningful development and stability. However, crimes and other illegal activities undermine public peace and security at any given time. It is therefore incumbent in the society to conduct effective policing to enhance national security. One of the major ways to achieve this much needed security of lives and property is by establishing Nation Police. Nation police is a key to sustainable security in Nigeria.

51. *Nation Police.* Nation policing entails the establishment of institutional mechanisms for the enforcement of laws to prevent conflicts and enhance peaceful co-existence among members of the society in the nation. In the United States of America (USA) there are two sets of police, FBI and State Police entrusted with powers of arrest. In US, citizens have limited powers of arrest if they see a crime being committed, usually referred to as "citizen's arrest". However, the common policing techniques in the US are FBI (Federal Bureau Intelligence) which is structurally centralised, more closely tied to central government and less accountable to either the public or the law. The state police is structurally organised within the state, more closely tied to the state government and less accountable to either the public or the law. They are however been successful in the USA.

52.   The South Africa Police Service also has a responsibility to prevent, protect property, combat and investigate crimes, maintain public law and order and secure the environment for all people in South Africa. The American and South African policing systems are backed with adequate welfare programmes, effective training, careful selection and logistic provision which have substantially enhanced national security in both countries.

53.   In Nigeria, members of the Nigeria Police Force (NPF) have statutory powers to investigate crimes, apprehend offenders, prosecute suspects, regulate or disperse processions and assemblies, search and seize properties suspected to be stolen or associated with crime. However, some inhibiting factors such as poor logistics, inadequate equipment, poor nationwide coverage and inadequate knowledge of the environment they are operating have continued to retard progressively policing functions to safeguard Nigeria's National Security. According to some scholars in Nigeria, the institutions and other mechanisms for controlling crimes and conflicts are either incapable of functioning appropriately because of the size of the country or are in dire need of a complete re-structure in order to foster policing and enhance Nigeria's national security.

54.   This chapter therefore, will discuss the effects of policing on national security in Nigeria. Accordingly, it will further clarify the key concepts of policing, national security and establish the relationship between them. It will also conduct an overview of policing on Nigeria's national security, identify issues, examine effects and highlight some challenges for Nigeria's national security before proffering strategies for the establishment of nation police in Nigeria. Nation police is very important and the time is ripe for it because there is no federation of Nigeria's size that does not have nation police. However, this section of the book on policing will cover years 2010 – 2017, being the period of various reforms in policing techniques in Nigeria towards improving national security yet there is no improvement with the attendance security challenges. It is against this backdrop of Nigeria's huge security challenges that nation police is mandatory. The aim of this chapter is to discuss the effects of nation policing on national security in Nigeria with a view to making recommendations.

CONCEPTUAL CLARIFICATION

55.   The key variables in this study are nation policing as the independent variable and national security as the dependent variable. These variables will be conceptualised and the relationship between them established.

Nation Police

56.   Nation Police is very important because there is no federation of Nigeria's size that does not have nation police. It is against this backdrop of Nigeria's huge security challenges that nation police is mandatory. In the United States, State Police are a police body unique to each US state, having state-wide authority to conduct Law enforcement activities and criminal investigations. Nation police formations would be more penetrative and wide spread touching the nooks and crannies of every community within the nation as well as community-friendly relative to the NPF. One of the reasons advanced by unpatriotic Nigerians against nation police is the fear of abuse of the force by governors, which critics had regularly held as part of the reasons for their opposition to the establishment of nation police. It remained untenable against the backdrop of the persisting allegations of the abuse of the NPF by those who currently run and control it.

National Security

57.   Luciani defines national security, "as the ability of a nation to withstand aggression from abroad". This definition views national security as security of the state and therefore not apt for this discussion. However, Enahoro believes that the definition of national security should accommodate all other goals such as freedom and welfare of the people.

58.   Obasanjo, supports this view by noting that the objective of national security ought to be to "advance the inherent aspirations of a country, to curtail instability, control crime and improve the welfare and quality of life of every citizen". He therefore defines national security as "the aggregation of the security interests of all individuals, communities, nations, ethnic groups, political entities and institutions, which inhabit the territory of our country". This section therefore

adopts Obasanjo's definition of national security as it encompasses the security dimensions and the welfare of all Nigerians.

RELATIONSHIP BETWEEN NATION POLICING AND NATIONAL SECURITY IN NIGERIA

59.   Nation policing focuses on security activities by an organised paramilitary force within the nation to keep the society safe from threat to lives and property through the enforcement of laws, values and ideologies to regulate the use of force. This implies that security of the people by the government is the main intent of state policing.

60.   However, national security viewed as freedom from danger and other factors that could threaten the legitimate interest, liberty and well being of the people. Therefore, the primary concern of national security is the safety of lives and property to the people and where these values are not safeguarded, national security of the people will be threatened. Hence, there exists a direct relationship between state policing and national security in Nigeria.

OVERVIEW OF NIGERIA POLICE FORCE ON NATIONAL SECURITY IN NIGERIA

61.   The history of the present day Nigeria Police Force (NPF) dates back to 1861 when a Consular Guard of 25 men was established in Lagos to protect British interests in the new colony. In 1862, a 500-member armed paramilitary constabulary called Hausa Constabulary was established. The Niger Coast Constabulary was also formed in Calabar in 1894 under the then newly proclaimed Niger Coast Protectorate to cater for the Eastern region. Likewise, in the North, the Royal Niger formed the Royal Niger Constabulary in 1886, with headquarter in Lokoja, to carter for the northern area. Subsequently, a Southern Police Forces was created in 1906. The Lagos Consular Guard (West), Hausa Constabulary (North) and Niger Coast Constabulary (East) which later became Southern Police Forces were later emerged in 1930 to form the NPF. These Western, Northern and Eastern Constabularies were then regional Police Forces. Presently, Section 214 of the Constitution of the Federal republic of Nigeria (CFRN), 1999 provides the legal status and constitutional authority for the NPF in maintaining law and order and protecting the citizenry.

62. The methods adopted for policing the entire country by the NPF include intelligence gathering, beat patrol, motorised patrol, stop and search, surveillance patrol among others. These policing methods were to ensure deterrence, assure peace, secure lives and properties, prevent and detect crimes, but they have not achieved satisfactory performances, which have continued to impact negatively on Nigeria's national security. The offences against persons and properties, armed robbery, kidnapping, ritual killings, herdsmen and insurgent activities have been on the increase. This could be corroborated by the crime returns, armed robbery returns, returns on property stolen/recovered due to armed robbery, kidnappings, returns of riots/civil disturbance, returns of agitations returns of, herdsmen and insurgents activities in Nigeria. The above increase in the criminal activities shows that the NPF policing methods have not achieved satisfactory success in crime prevention, control and detection thereby inhibiting national security hence the people's reason for advocating for state police for enhance peace and national security.

ISSUES OF NATION POLICE AND NATIONAL SECURITY IN NIGERIA

63. The issues of nation police and national security in Nigeria include policy for establishment, welfare and logistics, manpower capacity development and funding. These issues are further discussed as follows.

Policy for Establishment

64. The policy for the establishment of the nation policing has been a major setback for advancing the establishment of the nation police. The various stakeholders are disagreeing on the policy for the establishment of Nation Police in Nigeria based on their selfish agenda to continue to use Federal Police as a means to intimidate their political opponents.

65. One other reason common among these unpatriotic elements is the fear of abuse of the force by state governors, which critics had regularly held as part of the reasons for their opposition to the establishment of nation police formations, which remained untenable against the backdrop of the persisting allegations of the abuse of the NPF by those who currently run and control it. Nation Police formations would be more penetrative and widespread touching the nooks and crannies of every community as well as community-friendly relative to the NPF. Therefore, there is the urgent need for the policy makers to pass a bill at the national assembly for the establishment of the nation police for enhanced state-wide law enforcement and criminal investigation in Nigeria's national security.

Welfare and Logistics

66. The pay structure of NPF personnel has been found to be very poor, resulting in extortion at public highways and other forms of corruption in the NPF. The established welfare schemes of the NPF have also not benefited the personnel satisfactorily, leading to poor morale and motivation.

67. Communication equipment and vehicle are also not adequate and those available are poorly maintained, leading to frequent break-downs, even while in operations. Move over, Police Equipment Fund that was established in June 2006 to source for fund from the public and multinationals to support the NPF in the provision of vehicles, communication equipment and others policing needs lacks legal backing and has not achieve its objectives as accrued funds has mostly been expended on incidentals and not logistic needs. It could however be appropriate for the government to stop over stretching the NPF and allow it to man federal highways, protect federal infrastructure and provide federal intelligence. While the nation police would be funded by the nation government as well as the provision of welfare and logistics, in order to improve nation policing for enhance national security in Nigeria.

Manpower Capacity Development

68. The United Nations recommends one police officer for every 400 citizens. This figure is relatively significant under "standard temperature and pressure" where the rate of crimes is greatly reduced as opposed to the present day criminal activities. Nigeria with a population of about 180,000,000 has more than 450,000 police officers and a police to citizen ratio is 1 to 450, which is grossly inadequate for policing to guarantee national security in Nigeria. Moreover, due to inadequate training and poor weapon handling skills, manpower wastage, lack of adequate coverage has been high without corresponding replacement/recruitment.

69. The rate of personnel exit from the NPF from 2010 - 2017 was high, with 2013 being the highest, could probably be due to the implementation of the NPF Reforms, which recommended the exit of aged, indiscipline and unproductive police personnel. However, the corresponding constable recruitment for 2010 – 2017 with rapid increase in 2017 to meet currently security challenges in the country. In view of the aforementioned, shows a deficit of personnel which if replace or exceed would have aided policing in the country. Additionally, because of the peculiar nature of the country where nepotism, language, religion and tradition rain supreme as well as terrain make it almost impossible to guarantee national security in Nigeria. Therefore, there is the need for the nations in Nigeria to have their own police to meet up the challenges of insecurity to enhance Nigeria's national security.

Funding

70. Paucity of fund is a major issue hampering the efficiency of NPF. The FGN has not being able to meet the challenges affecting the NPF. This is noticeable in the manner in which NPF carry on their policing across the country with attendant increase in extortions and criminal activities.

71.   Additionally, looking at the population and Nigeria meagre resource the NPF would not be adequately run by FGN for crime prevention strategy. This continues to pose enormous challenges in crime prevention with the attendant effects on national security. Therefore, there is the need for the funding of police to rest on the shoulder of the nation government for effective policing to enhance Nigeria's national security.

EFFECTS OF NATION POLICING ON NATIONAL SECURITY IN NIGERIA

72.   The sustenance of the society is hinged on an efficient law enforcement process capable of shielding the society from the menace of criminality. However, on Nigeria's return to democratic rule in 1999, the NPF had generated, poorly armed and demoralised personnel that could not perform its constitutional roles satisfactorily. However, some identified effects of policing in Nigeria's national security are discussed below.

Crime Control and Prevention

73.   The NPF has not been successful in crime control and prevention, thus exhibiting glaring incapacity to effectively enforce laws and maintain order in Nigeria. More cases of robberies, arsons, assassinations, kidnapping, human rituals, child-theft herdsmen and insurgent activities amongst other vices, have continued unabated and as a result there is continuous rise in crime rates in Nigeria. However, this trend

could be curtailed through effective nation policing established by the individual nations to enhance Nigeria's national security.

Promotion of Local and Foreign Direct Investments

74. A crime free society would guarantee a favourable environment for both local and foreign direct investments. Conversely, the rising rate of crime has continued to impact negatively on investments thus depriving the country of accruable revenue with attendant losses to the economy. Effective nation policing would however enhance investments, create jobs and reduce unemployment thus engendering Nigeria's national security.

Promotion of Tourism.

75. The tourism industry in Nigeria has regressed due to the spate of bombings, kidnappings, robberies, vandalism, herdsmen and insurgent activities and other social vices pervading the country. However, potential tourists would desire a secured environment and safety of their lives and property. Effective nation policing if established would however reduce these crimes and guarantee the much needed security for potential tourists to travel to various locations across the country.

CHALLENGES MILITATING AGAINST POLICING FOR NATIONAL SECURITY IN NIGERIA

76. The challenges militating against NPF policing for national security in Nigeria include poor training, inadequate manpower, poor remuneration, infrastructure, and poor logistics for police personnel and more importantly lack of established nation police. These challenges are further discussed below.

Poor training and Inadequate Manpower

77.   Due to inadequate training facilities, majority of personnel are only exposed to enlistment training. This level of training is, however, grossly inadequate to cope with emerging challenges of national security. Also, the shortage of personnel has led to the excessive use of those available, mostly as guards and escorts to politicians and business moguls; leaving a few for policing, thus negatively impacting on national security. Moreover, NPF recruitment/enlistment has not matched the rate of exist hence poor coverage of the entire country to cover policing activity. Therefore, there is the need for nation police to handle policing activity in every nation in Nigeria for enhance national security in Nigeria.

Poor remuneration, Infrastructure and Logistics

78.   The monthly salary of police personnel remains irregular and grossly inadequate to meet the basic needs of life and maintain a family. Moreover, the Police Welfare Schemes such as the NPF Insurance Scheme and the Small Scale Credit Scheme had also been fraught with irregularities, thereby not realizing their set objectives. Accommodation, recreational facilities, communication equipment, vehicles, weapons, ammunitions and medical facilities are also inadequate for policing thereby endangering national security. Therefore, there is the need to establish nation police to take care of these inadequacies to localise policing activity for enhance national security.

Inadequate Community/Vigilante Policing

79. Vigilante or Community Policing, currently practiced in nations in Nigeria has been fairly satisfactory but general crime rate has not reduced due to the rising level of unemployment, inadequate logistics, and poor intelligence analysis amongst others. However, the non extension of Vigilante/Community Policing to other nations in Nigeria could be partly responsible for the rising rate of crime in those nations, thus impacting negatively on Nigeria's national security. Therefore, there is the need to establish proper nation police in every nation of the federation, with powers of arrest and prosecution to fight criminal activities in the nation for enhance national security in Nigeria.

STRATEGIES TO ENHANCE POLICING FOR NATIONAL SECURITY IN NIGERIA

80. The strategies to enhance policing for national security in Nigeria include human capacity development, improved remuneration and logistics and establishment of nation police in Nigeria. These strategies are discussed in succeeding paragraphs.

Human Capacity Development

81. Human capacity in the NPF could be restructured and developed by reviewing recruitment policies, training curricula and extending training facilities for quality increase in recruitment and enlistment. These recruits after training could be deployed to their nation of origin to form nation police. Also, the NPF, through enlightenment campaign and other human resources development training institutions develop validation tests for enlistment, further recruitment and training of policemen in their respective state will be continued by the nation. This could be achieved by the fourth quarter of 2020.

Improved Remuneration, Infrastructure Development and Logistics

82. The review and regular payment of salaries and allowances and benefits from other NPF Welfare Schemes would boost the morale of police personnel for more commitment to their duties. Also, the renovation and construction of barracks with modern recreational and workshop facilities, the provision of adequate logistic support for prevention and investigation of crimes would further boost the confidence of police personnel in crime prevention, control and prosecution of offenders within their nations. Some of these incentives would be better handled by the nation government which would relieve the pressure on FGN for enhanced nation policing in Nigeria. This could be achieved by the first quarter of 2021.

Establishment of Nation Police

83. Nation police have been found to be very effective in combating crimes in the UK, USA and Brazil among others. Nation Policing would be greatly successful if practiced in Nigeria because the Nation police personnel are familiar with overall terrain in their nation. Therefore, with adequate personnel deployment to their respective nation of origin for immediate take off of nation police, further training of recruits by nation police and logistic support, nation policing could achieve great success if established in all states of the federation in Nigeria. This could be achieved by the first quarter of 2020.

CONCLUSION

84. This book has briefly discussed the challenges of Nigeria before and after amalgamation, what went wrong, why and way forward. It has also tried to discuss in brief some of the issues in Nigeria Politics ranging from the pursuit of selfish agenda in Nigerian polity, insecurity, what is a nation and country and how nations and countries are made, poor leadership, poverty, poor governance and procedures to achieve good governance. This book noted the impact of free and fair election in politics, the importance of spirituality in nation's building. National character and way forward to ensure enhance national peace, stability and development in Nigeria.

85. The country since the era of independence to present had been experiencing intractable spate of disunity, civil unrest, violent crimes, armed robbery, different levels of agitations, bombing, kidnapping, failure of government policies and presently herdsmen and insurgents activities among others. This book noted that the impact of these crimes to national security has assumed critical dimensions which require the implementation of appropriate strategies to enhance national security.

86. The book also identified poor training, inadequate manpower, poor remuneration, infrastructure and logistics and inadequate coverage and lack of nation police as challenges to policing in Nigeria. To overcome the indentified challenges, the book proffered some strategies. These include constitution overhaul, regional autonomy, confederation system, and nation policing and a more efficient implementation of separation of powers to enhance Nigeria's national security. It is worthy of note that the Northern, western and Eastern Nigeria were joined together in the first place by Lord Lugard because of perceived threats from French colonies surrounding these regions or nations. Lord Lugard amalgamated (union) the three nations out of fear of the unknown, if there's any attack on any one of the nations it will be an attack on all. It is also clear today that the threat is no longer visible and secondly, these regions or nations are not making any progress in their union therein. Therefore, it is suggested that the best bet and most appropriate thing to do is to dissolve the union to enhance peace, stability and development in the region, if all the issues affecting their cooperate existence or unity cannot be fully addressed. This union dissolve is well recognised under the principles of self-determination which is duly provided for in both United Nation Charter on Rights of Ingenious People and African Charter on Human and Peoples Rights.

RECOMMENDATIONS

87. It is recommended that Nigeria must:

a. Return to the constitution at independence which our founding fathers (Colonial masters) bequeathed to Nigeria.

b. Return to the constitution that allowed the nations or regions autonomy in the management of their affairs.

c. The nations/regions will be federating units with its own rights to have their constitution.

d. The nations/regions will have control of its resources and make agreed contribution to the federal government (centre) for general services as its being practised in USA and other developed countries in the world.

e. The nations/regions should be allowed to have their own police for the protection of the nation/region.

f. Any Nigeria residing in any parts of the country is bounded by the constitution of the nation/region in which he is residing.

g. The Nigerian Military must return to its constitutional role of defence of territorial integrity of Nigeria; defence against external threats and may be called upon by nation/region to assist in event of natural disaster or insecurity which the nation/region cannot handle through the Federal government.

h. The name of Nigeria should be changed to read United Republic of Nigeria as proposed by the Colonial masters because the 3 nations that made up Nigeria were amalgamated (united) by Lord Lugard for a purpose or reason of the Bigger the Better without recourse to the consent of its diverse nations.

i. That the United Republic of Nigeria should be fashioned or operated in line with what is obtainable in the United Kingdom or USA where every nation will be administered independently.

j. That the federal government should be responsible for the administration of the Military, Federal Police, Foreign Affairs and Home Land Security.

k. Nigeria must back track to join the direction that leads to destiny if she must survive as a United Republic.

l. Hausa, Ibo and Yoruba nations were joined together as a union in the first place because of the perceived threats from French colonies. Since the threats are no longer visible and the Hausa, Ibo and Yoruba nations are not making any meaningful progress in their union then the best bet and most appropriate thing to do is to dissolve the union for enhance peace, stability and development in the region.

m. The Union dissolve is well recognised under the principle of self-determination which is duly provided for in both United Nations Chatter on Rights of Indigenous People and Africa Chatter on Human and Peoples Rights.

n. Nations are progressive not only on human thoughts but also on genuine spiritual drive. Genuine spirituality is germane to nation building.

o. For fairness and equity, the federal government must set up a standing commission to carter for promotion in the military and MDA comprising equal numbers of representatives from the regions, as opposed to one man deciding the future of personnel under command which lays foundation for inequality, injustice and unfairness which is the bed rock for corruption in Nigeria.

p. Where all these cardinal points cannot be attained in both truth and faith then there is the need for Nigeria to disintegrate because the centre can no longer hold. There is strength in smaller the stronger.

q. Nigeria is a signatory to the Rights of Self-determination as contained in the United Nations Chatter.

r. The three nations that made up Nigeria were amalgamated the same day, same time and same moment. Therefore no one nation will want to claim ownership of Nigeria or dominate the others except that one nation wants to start second local colonization of others which is a mission impossible. Nigeria is a union of 3 nations and can break up if their reason for the union can no longer be attained or hold and or if any one nation feels isolated or marginalised by the other or others. It is a matter of choice for one to be part of a union not by force. The nations are joined to form a union peacefully and so shall it pull out of it peacefully without any hindrance or fear of molestation or attack. After all, all nations all over the world that were amalgamated to become countries were done out of FEAR of the UNKNOWN.